SEERS
HANDBOOK

By

Sharnael Wolverton

Endorsements

"Sharnael Wolverton has a passion to see the kingdom of God extended through prophecy, signs and wonders. With her bold, simple faith in action, she is blazing a trail for many to follow."

Stacey Campbell
Revival Now! Ministries

In a time when a generation needs connection with God's Spirit, Sharnael is uniquely gifted to provide. Her sincere desire to train people and reach out is infused with God's love, grace, and compassion.

Doug Addison
InLight Connection

"I am struck by several things in Sharnael, but especially her hunger for God and her passion for the prophetic. Her desire to see the supernatural poured out in the earth is very refreshing. Sharnael is truly a "Daughter of Destiny" called to impact her generation for God."

Larry Randolph
Larry Randolph Ministries

"This is the year of Sharnael's rising! This is her running year!"

Graham Cooke
Future Training Institute

"The church is in a fresh new day. Divine opportunities are at the door in an unprecedented way. Likewise, there are also many new and fresh faces emerging with holy desperation in their soul and passion for God's kingdom. Sharnael Wolverton of Swiftfire Ministries International is one such example!"

Paul Keith Davis
WhiteDove Ministries

"Sharnael has been called to preach, teach and prophesy, there is an apostolic seed of anointing inside of her and she has a prophet's mantle upon her. The working of her faith will cause a response from the Heavens!"

Patricia King
Extreme Prophetic

SEERS HANDBOOK

By

Sharnael Wolverton

swiftfire publishing
1113 S. Range Ave. Suite 110, Box 333 Denham Springs, La 70726
225-791-7696 swiftfire.org

International Standard Book Number:
978-09796622-1-8
First Printing June 2007

Editor: Arlene Brown
Contributing Editor: Charlotte Bouzigard
Cover Graphics: Sharnael and Stephen Wolverton
Cover Image: Ashley Carriere
Eagle Images: Robert Bartow Bartowimages.com
Interior Design: Don Pennington

Printed in the United States of America

To contact the author about speaking at your church or conference or
For more information on swiftfire resources go to
www.swiftfire.org

Published By
swiftfire publishing
Denham Springs, LA 70726

Dedications

To Shiloh and Seraphina

Foreword

Sharnael offers something needed for the church: a fresh perspective with new inventive ideas that awaken people to how deep the kingdom of God can really be. She has a prophetic perspective about both the church world and the secular world. Her supernaturally natural Biblical presentation in her meetings coupled with her writing style set her apart in this day where people are longing for not just new voices but a radical cry of intimacy and reality of who God really is.

Shawn Bolz
Expression58 Ministries

Foreword

Some are gifted with a *prophetic message* for their hour; others have a *prophetic gift* and can speak a personal word over your life with great accuracy. Sharnael is that rare person with a *prophetic life*, which includes both a message to the hour and a gift for personal ministry. Combined with her prophetic acumen, Sharnael's single minded, whole hearted devotion to Jesus makes her a trusted voice in my life and one I encourage others to listen to as well.

Lance Wallnau
Lancelearning Group

Table of Contents

Chapter		Page
1	The Seer Anointing	13
2	Body Parts	15
3	Fruit	29
4	Numbers	33
5	Colors	35
6	Miscellaneous Symbols	37
7	Your Own Spiritual Vocabulary	41
	About the Author	59

The Seer Anointing

God speaks in many ways. This book came from years of adding to my many lists within countless journals of symbols and signs from God. These revelations came from dreams, visions and various spiritual encounters. Many of these symbols come to me when ministering to other people.

The seer anointing is a wonderful thing. For more explanation of a seer and the seer anointing, I recommend doing a word study from your bible to get the full meaning.

I also encourage you to read Jim Goll's book "*The Seer*" as it provides great understanding of the various functions of a seer in great detail.

Jim's book also gives scriptural and historic background to the seer. (www.swiftfire.org to order).

But for those of you reading this now, for the sake of time, I will assume that I am speaking to people who already know what a seer is and I will provide some examples of the different ways the Lord speaks to me personally whether in prayer, ministry or in dreams.

One type manifestation of the seer anointing is the supernatural ability to use the five senses. In other words, the ability to hear, see, touch, smell, and feel under the influence and anointing of God and the power of the Holy Spirit. Many times God uses pictures or symbols to help us comprehend what He wants to say. This book provides some of the symbols He has used in my life.

I hope these symbols help you. You may not understand or agree with me. This is okay. This is my language. You will have yours. Like I said in the beginning God speaks in *many* ways.

I pray that as you read these pages that God would impart more understanding and revelation to you regarding the language He so longs for us to know—the language of the spirit. The language of love!

Body Parts

Often times when I am praying for people I will get weird sensations in my body.

Sometimes, it will feel like pain. Sometimes, it's a numb feeling or tingling feeling.

Other times, I will just feel the wind of the Spirit over my own body part or parts indicating an emphasis to what the Lord is saying regarding that particular organ.

These sensations are one way that the Lord will speak to me regarding the person I am ministering to.

As I pray, the pain/numbness lifts once the prayers are spoken and finished in the spirit.

These symbols have been collected over a period of years and may give you some insight as to how He speaks to you.

Please keep in mind, this list is always being added to and sometimes it even changes. So, please do not *always* count on this list as *your* own personal truth or language. It is to be used as a guide.

__Ankle/Ankles__—helps hold the legs in balance providing a steady walk. Many times while praying for people I have seen or felt shackles around the ankles. This is an indication to me that the person is being bound from their full potential, and their spiritual walk is being hindered. I often pray for a breakthrough release for the person to be set free into their full destiny.

__Arm/Arms__—authority, strength; the right arm refers to what the person has faith to do. The left arm is about what they are born to do or destined to do.

__Back__—speaks of alignment, apostolic, your frame connecting the body, keeping the whole body in position or in line; Strength. An attack against the back can be an attack against the calling to an apostolic ministry or it can be an attack against things lining up for your life or for your ministry/family/life.

Breast—nourishment, to nourish someone else, spiritual connotation: to bring or receive a teaching. To bring comfort to help mature. Attacks against the breasts are attacks against the ability to nourish, teach, comfort or help bring to maturity.

Bad milk or nourishment means false teaching or bad teaching. Also, false comfort.

Cheek—forgiveness; "to turn the other cheek."
To forgive or to have unforgiveness.

Chin—to take a hit, "taking it on the chin" Strength. Examine your attitude "Chin up."

Ear/Ears—listening, spiritual listening, deafness physically or spiritually. Negative words spoken, seed or seeds of negativity within your ears. Balance-inner ear problems could mean a shift is here, a change for the positive or for the negative.

Eye/Eyes— spiritual sight, physical sight, vision, seer anointing, frame of vision, spiritual cleanliness:

Matthew 6:22—23

The eye is the lamp of the body. If your eyes are good, your whole body will be full of light. But if your eyes are bad, your whole body will be full of darkness.

Eyebrow/Eyebrows/Eyelashes—protection for the eye and eye gate spiritually.

Face—intimacy, "in-to-me-see." Attack or blow to the face is an attack against intimacy or an attack against the senses. (Seer anointing)

Fingers—five-fold ministry.

Pinky Finger— teacher, teaching anointing. Teachers bring the Word with great understanding and have an insatiable desire to study and teach the Word. This is the finger that gets into the ear of the people and best brings balance to the five-fold ministry.

Ring Finger—the wedding finger, pastoral calling, married to the church or bride, closest to the heart.

Middle Finger—evangelism, the gathering finger, reaches out further than the other fingers to touch people.

Point Finger—to have a prophetic call or anointing or to point out the prophetic call or anointing. Not to point out faults! This gifting is meant to guide in the correct direction, pointing the way. (For additional insight read, *"Keys to Third Heaven Using Third Heaven Revelation to Impact a World"*).

Thumb Finger—apostolic call or anointing, holds all the fingers together in a fist. Keeps everyone balanced and together.

An attack against any of these fingers could also be an attack against the call or anointing on your life to serve in these functions. Slamming finger in a door, or missing a finger for whatever reason…

Arthritis—pray against the attack of the five-fold ministry in general and the joint positions for these functions…can also indicate a call to pray and intercede for body.

__Foot/Feet__—peace and beauty:

Isaiah 52:7

How beautiful on the mountains are the feet of those who bring good news, who proclaim peace, who bring good tidings, who proclaim salvation.

May refer to your walk, your conduct. Again, there are times I have seen shackles on a persons ankles causing people not to be able to walk forward in their potential. If you encounter this in a ministry setting, ask the Holy Spirit to break the powers of darkness and ask God for a release in the destiny of that person.

__Lame Foot__— unhealthy reliance on those who are undependable or unfaithful.

Proverbs 25:19

Like a bad tooth or a lame foot is reliance on the unfaithful in times of trouble.

__Gut__—discernment, a knowing in the pit of your stomach. Can mean a strong need for discernment or a strong gift of discernment.

Hair—your covering or accountability. Hair can represent strength but can also represent religion and mans traditions. Hair cuts are good, and may show that you had some things cut off (in the spirit) that needed to come off. Hair cuts can also represent covenant with God. (Paul's Nazarene vow).

Hand/Hands—action, service, works, covenant (handshake), hands hold the five-fold ministry. Clean hands represent clean works, hot hands can mean a healing anointing. Hands may also represent giving, being generous, open hands, a place of receiving, open to Holy Spirit or in need of help.

Head—authority, government, an attack on the head (headache or migraine) can mean witchcraft and oppression coming against you and your "frame of mind." An attack of the mind to steal your peace and give you stress. Break the witchcraft and oppression coming against you or the person you are ministering to.

Heart—emotions, heart motives, discernment, love walk, life.

Heel—a place of weakness. Ask for supernatural protection and wisdom for the person you are ministering to.

Hip—carries new beginnings (babies), loves to pioneer new things and carry them no matter how heavy. Someone who "shoots from the hip," means someone who is very honest and speaks their mind. (Sometimes in wisdom but this is not always the case). Hips also represent bringing balance to one's walk.

Jaw—strength, power, tension, strife, or repetition in prayers (religious behavior).

Knee/Knees—humility, humble, bended knee. Often a person with a strong prayer life or a call to prayer for a specific season or function. An attack in the knee or knees would be an attack against prayer life or it can indicate humility issues.

Kidney/Kidneys—the place where the anointing comes from, the reins, the place where power comes from: healing, miracles, apostolic gifting or function. The organ that helps filter the body. This seems to be a common attack against those with an apostolic call or healing/miracles ministry.

Leg/Legs—your walk, faith. Again, your left side refers to the faith of what you are born to do. The right side is what you have faith for today.

Mouth/Lips/Speech—your testimony, or your calling to speak, sing, teach, preach or deliver a message. Any attack against these areas or the throat could be an attack against your call in these ministry functions.

"Big mouth" represents someone who cannot control his mouth, gossip. "Stiff upper lip" often means that someone is tough or has had to be tough because a lot of responsibility has been put on them. Or perhaps someone who has had to maintain a tough image or life style.

A numbing of the upper lip can mean a softness is coming where the person you are ministering to will not have to have such a stiff upper lip. They will not have to be so tough because God is stepping in.

Neck—holds the head up, holds the head in place, authority. Also, a place of stubbornness, as in "stiff necked," or "a pain in the neck." Tension in the neck can mean they have been walking in some tense situations or sometimes even in pride. But please do not say that to the person! Release the opposite! Release new levels of love which is the opposite of pride. (Pride is a fear of looking bad). So, you release love because it is the opposite of fear. Also, release the person in peace to cancel all tense situations or strife in their life.

Nose—discernment, the ability to just "know" things. It isn't a hearing or seeing gifting but rather a knowing within without having to really think about it. Having a big nose in the spirit would indicate a generous gift of discernment.

Ribs/Chest— the protection of the emotions and heart. (Spiritually it could be a healthy protection or an unhealthy protection). The chest also can often carry heaviness, i.e. "an elephant is on my chest," meaning there is something wrong or uncomfortable in the spirit or in the natural. There is a block of the freedom to breathe, and no flow of the Holy Spirit. If you see a "puffed up" chest you are probably sensing pride issues. Again, release love to the person, which is the opposite of fear. (Pride is often rooted in fear). Also, release revelation of the truth.

Shoulder/Shoulders—can represent government or authority; burden bearer. Burden bearing can be a positive thing as sometimes God asks us to take things on in prayer, but sometimes these burdens take on a life of their own if not given over in prayer for God to take what isn't meant to be carried. If you are feeling pain or discomfort in the area of the shoulders, break off any false burdens and ask for the fresh revelation of Him carrying our every load or weight.

Skin—tough calloused skin represents a tough outer protection guarding the inside emotions. Someone who has been deeply wounded; (Wounded people wound other people). Tender, soft skin is a representation of a countenance reflecting the throne of Glory. It may also refer to the beautiful, healthy protection of the body.

Teeth—teeth represent wisdom. Teeth represent our ability to chew on the word of God and or decisions. Fear of losing one's teeth can also mean a fear of not having ability to make correct decisions. Actually losing teeth would be losing the ability to make good decisions.

Eye Teeth—our ability to see spiritually.

Cavities—represent a need to get clarity in order to make good healthy decisions.

Fillings-can indicate a lot of poor choices and

unhealthy reliance on those who are unfaithful and undependable.

Proverbs 25:19

Like a bad tooth or lame foot is reliance on the unfaithful in times of trouble.

<u>*Veneers*</u> —a false sense of wisdom, looks good but not real.

There can also be false teeth (false wisdom) and baby teeth (immaturity). Losing baby teeth would be a graduation of sorts into more maturity more wisdom.

<u>*Crooked Teeth*</u>—would mean there needs to be some alignment or braces to straighten out some mind sets.

<u>*Thigh*</u>—your faith or your walk; Can also can represent a wrestling with God about a particular issue or lifestyle.

<u>*Throat*</u>—a tightening of the throat or a feeling of being strangled can mean that a witchcraft curse is

coming against the person. A python spirit often manifests with a feeling of strangling or suffocating. Break the power of any evil force coming against the person and release freedom to breathe and move in the Holy Spirit. A sore throat or a consistent sore throat represents an attack against the calling to speak truth, teach, preach, sing or deliver a message.

Toe/Toes—bring balance and help your walk. Often times my big toe will buzz meaning the person has a strong understanding of the need for balance in their life. If there is pain in the toe it can mean they probably need balance in their life or in a particular area of their life. An attack against the toe (stubbing your toe, toenail coming off, etc.) would represent an attack against balance or a need for more protection in the area of balance.

Womb— represents birthing, the place where a new beginning takes place. I have often witnessed people who have birthed something in the spirit. It has only happened to me once. It felt like real contractions.

I also know certain people in ministry who have a healing anointing for fertility. A word of caution: be careful prophesying in the area of babies and births. It is a touchy subject unless you absolutely know it is God promising a child to the person in the near future. Wombs also represent a place of bearing fruit, both good and bad fruit.

Wrist/Wrists—the part of the body that helps hold the hand or five-fold ministry. Strength in general; Strength to give and be generous. At times, I have prayed for people and felt shackles on my wrists or could see shackles on the person I was ministering to. This can mean the enemy was trying to hold the person back from moving forward in their potential. Break the evil fetters that bind the person and ask for a breakthrough release.

Fruit

Frequently I smell fruit or see fruit over different people as I minister. These symbols may not be everyone's language but if you desire to move more in a seer anointing you can ask the Lord to help you smell or see more in the spirit and give you revelation regarding what comes to you.

Apples—peace and health. The "apple of His eye." (Deuteronomy 32:10 and Zechariah 2:8). Freedom from distraction and disturbing thoughts. Apples can also represent a perfect word for a perfect time.

Apples can also symbolize sin or temptation.

Bananas—gentleness, softness, tender. A gentle hearted servant; bananas contain potassium, which is good for the heart and brain. It builds the heart up and prevents twisting, aching muscles in the body. Bananas can also refer to conduct and presentation.

Grapes—faithfulness, loyal to the Lord, no other options considered.. Saying "No" to all options and temptations except God's. We may think of grapes as being little here on earth, but in heaven and in the promised land they are *huge* taking two or more men to carry them!

Grapes also represent ingredients for the new wine and new wine skins needed to keep with God. When you smell grapes you can bet there is a shift in the life/ministry/person or church for the better! And a death to the old!

Grapefruit—sweet and sour, a constant dying to self is evident. Person is fighting with self control and selfish behaviors but continuously trying to overcome. They are loyal to the Lord and yearn for the old man to die once and for all.

Lemons—sour; a poor sport. Not open.

Oranges—sweet companionship with the Lord. The person spends much time in the "Son." Sweet aroma to the Lord. The kiss of God; even the "sun" kiss of God!

__Peaches__—joy; sweet, sense of well being. A sense that the person is truly pleasing to the Lord. The Lord rejoices in them!

__Pears__—long life. Pear trees have long life enduring much without complaining. Bears good fruit.

__Tomatoes__—kindness, the heart of God; Big hearted, very generous. One who sows generously. No trouble hearing from God. One without any guile or defilement.

__Strawberries__—goodness, excellence in nature and virtue. Healing; sweet and very humble. Don't have to be big to be used. Doesn't have to be seen.

Numbers

1 God
2 Double/Multiplication/Justice/Established
3 The Trinity
4 Creative Works/Four corner of earth
5 Grace
6 Man
7 Perfectly Complete and Whole/Full
8 New Beginnings Teacher
9 Judgments Evangelist
10 Wilderness/Temptation/Trial/Pastor
11 Transition/Prophet
12 Apostolic Government
13 Rebellion/Revolution
14 Double Anointing/Perfect/Established
15 Grace Grace Grace
16 Established New Beginning
30 Beginning Ministry or Call
40 Wilderness Ends
50 Jubilee
111 My Beloved Son
666 Mark of Beast

Colors

<u>Black</u> — evil sin or all the color anointings mixed together.

<u>Brown</u> — humility or humanity

<u>Blue</u> — revelation or depression

<u>Gold/Yellow</u>— health, strength, fear

<u>Green</u> — growth, maturity, wealth, envy

<u>Orange</u>— son kiss, perseverance, danger

<u>Pink</u> — anointing on all flesh, innocence

<u>Purple</u> — royalty or pride

<u>Red</u> — wisdom or passion

<u>Silver</u>—redemption

<u>White</u> —holy, pure, or religious spirit

Miscellaneous

Here is another list of miscellaneous symbols that the Lord often gives me:

Arrows —I sometimes see arrows in a person's back when praying for them. When this happens God is letting me know this person is a wounded warrior.

In other words, the person has had fiery darts shot at them. Sometimes they are from witchcraft, other times they can be curses. Sometimes they come from words spoken against them; either personally to their face or behind their backs.

(If I see the arrows in the person's back, then the negative words are coming from behind their back. The victim may not even know they have been shot. The wounded feel the pain emotionally and sometimes even physically but may not know why they feel so terrible). I remove the arrows prophetically and ask for healing for the wounds releasing them into new and fresh ground.

Golden Pen —when I see a golden pen over the head of the person I minister to I know that they have a gift for writing. It may be music, books, poetry, teachings or sermons. I encourage them to continue and pray for them.

Sometimes they do not even know they have the gift. When I know this is true, I will prophetically take the pen and hand it to thcm while explaining their gifting. This usually activates the gifting and stirs the person to excitement within their heart to "pen" for Him.

Hook/Hooks— I often see hooks in the hearts of those needing a release from the past, past hurts or from certain "pet" sins. I ask the Lord to remove the hooks and replace them with an anchor of His love. I also ask the Lord to give the person a fresh revelation of His love because when His love is in your heart you do not even *want* to sin against Him no matter the temptation.

Keys—when I see a key or multiple keys for someone, I know they are receiving new revelation. I ask the Lord to give them wisdom to apply the revelation being imparted. They also may be receiving a new found ability to go places they have never gone before both in the natural and in the spirit.

Musical Notes —when I see musical notes I know the person has a call to play music, write music, or sing. I ask the Lord to blow fresh creativity over them in order for them to fulfill the call on their life.

Tornados— tornados and twisters around people or over people represent confusion the person may be facing. It can also mean chaos and terrible trials the person is currently caught in the middle of. I pray to the Lord and ask the God of Breakthrough to come and calm the storms in their life. I ask for curses and witchcraft to be broken and ask the confusion to be dispelled.

These are just a few. I hope this will help you and start the quest for your own symbol language with Him.

I encourage you to ask for revelation everyday to better understand His spirit-to-spirit language.

You'll receive tremendous revelation when you stay in His word, too, so read His Word and watch the spirit come to life in new ways.

The last thing I strongly encourage you to do is to read my book titled *"Keys to Third Heaven...Using Third Heaven Revelation to Impact a World." (Go to www.swiftfire.org for more information).*

This book contains many powerful revelations regarding the area of ministry and the supernatural results we *can* have when functioning in ministry *God's way.*

This teaching came to me within a series of dreams and visions regarding these issues.

Please check it out and watch the power you currently walk in increase! These revelations will help you to shift the world around you for the kingdom!

God Bless your journey!

His,
Sharnael

Your Own Spiritual Vocabulary

Your Own Spiritual Vocabulary

Your Own Spiritual Vocabulary

Your Own Spiritual Vocabulary

Your Own Spiritual Vocabulary

Your Own Spiritual Vocabulary

Prophetic Evangelism

If you are interested in hosting a prophetic evangelism workshop or to get more training in this area, please go to www.swiftfire.org or email info@swiftfire.org for more information.

Testimony Time

If you have any testimonies as a result of reading this book, please let us know! We would love to hear from you!

Send your testimonies to info@swiftfire.org. Or write to:

Swiftfire Ministries International
1113 S. Range Ave
Ste 110 Box 333
Denham Springs, LA 70726
www.swiftfire.org

We are very interested in what God is doing through your lives as a result of this book.

Sharnael Wolverton

foreword by Joy Parrott

Keys
to
Third Heaven

Using Third Heaven Revelation to Impact a World

Dreams, Visions, Impartation & Activation to the Realms of the Spirit World

Join Sharnael in this revolutionary teaching uncovering key truths within the supernatural. You, too, can shift the world with these innovative revelations!

If you want to see, hear, understand and move in power like never before this book is for you!

For more information on this product and more, visit swiftfire.org

We are the Bionic Bride! We are the ones called to do GREATER THINGS than Jesus did! We are all born supernatural beings! We just need to believe and understand what that looks like for us!

Join Sharnael in this teaching providing insight on how we, too, can step into the call of God on our lives in the arena of the supernatural.

For more information on this product and more, visit swiftfire.org

This cd is full of dreams, visions, impartation and
activation to the realms of the spirit world.

Join Sharnael in this popular teaching uncovering
key truths in the areas of the prophetic. You, too, can
shift the world with these innovative revelations!
If you want to hear, see and understand like never
before this cd is for you!

For more information on this product and more,
visit swiftfire.org

Everyone needs help defeating the religious spirit.
The good news is with His help we can! In this two
part series Sharnael shares revelation on both how to
identify the religious spirit and how to overcome its
tactics in order to experience a life of victory and
freedom in the Holy Spirit!

For more information on this product and more,
visit swiftfire.org

On this journey, we have all had and will have bumps
in the road. Whether we are facing financial
problems, illness, the loss of a child, parent, or spouse,
divorce or other real issues, sooner or later there
must be a breakthrough! Sharnael's teaching
"Shaking to Groundbreaking" provides understanding
on how to find peace in the midst and how to
press in through the "shaking" in order to reach
the "groundbreaking!"

For more information on this product and more,
visit swiftfire.org

Some of us are called to be trail blazers, pioneers,
trend setters, REVOLUTIONISTS! Sharnael's
teaching "Spirit of a Revolutionist" gives inside
understanding to this precious call! Dive in and see
the power of God revolutionize your life!

For more information on this product and more,
visit swiftfire.org

"What is Breakthrough" provides hope and courage
to those in a place of desperately needing change
for their situation! Listen and receive necessary
words of life to revive your soul!

For more information on this product and more,
visit swiftfire.org

Plan Now to Attend Our Next Louisiana AmpliFIRE Conference!

Sharnael Wolverton and the Swiftfire Ministries International team welcome you to come and receive ministry from the Holy Spirit at one of our meetings here in Louisiana.

It is a great time of awesome worship, prophetic kingdom messages and personal ministry time! It is a wonderful time to encounter Him as well as meet new friends.

Make time to get away from your busy schedule and be rejuvenated in His presence!

For more information about our next meeting visit our website at:

www.swiftfire.org

Swiftfire Ministries International Information:

God's vision for Swiftfire Ministries International is that we would effectively help people recognize who they are in Christ and to guide them into the fullness of who they are. This is done in order for each one to carry out the purposes of God moment to moment.

Swiftfire's mission is to do this through: itinerant ministry, conferences, schools, workshops, mission trips, outreaches, prophetic evangelism, dream interpretation, counseling, intercession, bible study, discipleship, media, music, dance, art, and both personal and team ministry.

Sharnael also feels God is calling us to a place of more unity within the body. She desires to network and connect leaders, pastors, itinerants, churches, mission groups, and "marketplace missionaries" not only in the U.S., but internationally. **Kingdom unity and relationship is key for effective change.**

For More Information:
Swiftfire Ministries International
1113 S Range Ave
STE 110 Box 333
Denham Springs, LA 70726   www.swiftfire.org

Booking Information

If you would like to book Sharnael Wolverton for your next conference, church meeting or retreat, please contact her at the address below. If you would like to become a "Fire Starter" (A Swiftfire Ministries International Partner) please contact us at:

Swiftfire Ministries International
1113 S Range Ave
STE 110 Box 333
Denham Springs, LA 70726

www.swiftfire.org
info@swiftfire.org

About the Author

Sharnael Wolverton of Swiftfire Ministries International was called to the ministry at an early age. In her pursuit for God, she went into a place of "the school of the Holy Spirit." During this period of seeking intimacy with Him, she encountered many dreams, visions, visitations, and divine appointments leading to the birthing of Swiftfire Ministries International. As she continues to lean into Him, she ministers and teaches under the prophetic anointing, causing revelation, activation, miracles, signs and wonders, and healing.

Sharnael not only has a heart for Kingdom ministry and training though speaking at conferences, teaching workshops, writing and hosting her television show "Swiftfire with Sharnael Wolverton" she also has a focus and heart for the war on poverty. Her passion for orphans, widows, and single mothers has been a driving force behind her fundraising to help in the area of these people groups.

Locally, since she is strategically located north of New Orleans, Louisiana, there have been awesome opportunities for ministry to those post hurricane Katrina and Rita victims. Many have relocated and started over in the area she currently resides. These people are very much still in need.

Internationally, she has been involved in several mission team groups over the last two decades and continues to raise support with a goal of establishing ten orphanages (Partnering with Wes and Stacey Campbell).

Sharnael is very excited about the potential of the ever changing "New Church" and all fresh ways the church can reach out. She offers both financial and governmental leadership support to "out of the box" coffee shop churches, home groups, media churches, new church plants and training centers. She equally supports the radiant "traditional" churches. Both variety and creativity are crucial to reach the world.

If you are interested in becoming a financial partner or prayer partner for any of these areas of her ministry please go to the website at www.swiftfire.org to learn more. Or write to info@swiftfire.org.